THINK SMALL
GROW BIG

THINK SMALL GROW BIG

A Social Media Survival Guide
for the Marketing Professional

AB KUIJER

IARLA BYRNE, TRANSLATOR

COSIMO BOOKS

NEW YORK

Cover design by Sanneke Prins
Interior design by www.popshopstudio.com

ISBN: 978-1-61640-540-3

Cosimo aims to publish books that inspire, inform, and engage readers worldwide. We use innovative print-on-demand technology that enables books to be printed based on specific customer needs. This approach eliminates an artificial scarcity of publications and allows us to distribute books in the most efficient and environmentally sustainable manner. Cosimo also works with printers and paper manufacturers who practice and encourage sustainable forest management, using paper that has been certified by the FSC, SFI, and PEFC whenever possible.

Ordering Information:
Cosimo publications are available at online bookstores. They may also be purchased for educational, business, or promotional use:
Bulk orders: Special discounts are available on bulk orders for reading groups, organizations, businesses, and others.
Custom-label orders: We offer selected books with your customized cover or logo of choice.

For more information, contact us at:

Cosimo, Inc.
P.O. Box 416, Old Chelsea Station
New York, NY 10011

info@cosimobooks.com

or visit us at:
www.cosimobooks.com

To my mother & father

TABLE OF CONTENTS

SOCIAL MEDIA: THE NEW WAY TO COMMUNICATE WITH YOUR CUSTOMERS

"Finally, you're going to write a book!" For many years, I have been getting hints that I should do more in terms of writing than just my daily blogs. The reason that I have started this book now— and successfully finished it despite my own time constraints and pressures—is that the time is right to get my thoughts on paper.

I UNDERSTAND HOW MARKETING PROFESSIONALS are constantly grappling with questions about stagnating sales or why their recruitment drives are ineffective. They want to know how one can best use social media as a panacea for these problems, especially where to start. Social media is unfortunately not a quick-fix solution to miraculously boost your sales. Social media can be used as another way of dealing with clients, at least in a different manner than that used over the last 20 years. My opinions are all in this handy guidebook. It is obviously far from complete insofar as there are many books dealing with Twitter, Facebook, and LinkedIn in nano-detail. I have decided not to go into such detail—I know that your time is precious and that there are only 24 hours in a day; information should be manageable and above all, it should be clear and pragmatic.

Although the advertising industry has changed drastically over its history, it is clear that the best advertisements are those that appeal to the consumer in a more intimate way—those that tell a story or make the viewer laugh or cry. Advertising that I always admired: the Fido Dido (7UP) refrigerator magnets, the tough and cool Marlboro cowboy commercials, the song, "I'd Like to Teach the World to Sing" from happy hippy people walking up a mountain drinking Coca-Cola. This advertising was fun, talked to the viewers in a meaningful way, gave them that happy-go-lucky feeling. We even played a game at home while we were watching commercials on TV: if you recognized the brand at the beginning of an ad, you had to scream loudly the name of the advertiser, "Colgaaaaate!" Those were some great brand experiences. The same type of experience should translate into social networking.

As the world of communications today intensifies and evolves, marketers are realizing the importance of social media. The only question is how to make social media work for you. How do you use LinkedIn, Twitter, and Facebook, how do you make it grow in tandem with your organizational needs, and how do you manage the feedback and responses from your clients? The purpose of *Think Small, Grow Big* is to offer a pragmatic explanation of the increasingly important role of social media and why old-fashioned advertising is becoming less effective.

Despite how much we all love advertising, we cannot deny that commercial messaging has become a nuisance in the daily life of the consumer. Television series like *24* are better watched on DVD since the broadcast of an episode on TV guarantees more commercials than Jack Bauer can shoot off bullets. We have all become somewhat advertising averse with pop-up blockers, spam email folders, do-not-call lists, and unlisted telephone numbers. It has even become the norm to treat commercial breaks as bathroom breaks.

This consumer behavior does not help advertisers get their messages across. Of course, the media agencies will think differently: "You have to buy more commercial airtime!" In addition, people also have to deal with all the spam in their inboxes, bombarding them with countless offers. All these unsolicited commercial messages are bad promotion for advertising. It's not surprising that consumers communicate with each other through social networks. The inbox becomes a place for messages from strangers and advertisers—messages you do not want to read. In general, young people were the first to adapt to the changes in web 2.0 and see email as something for an older generation. To get around this, advertisers have begun using SMS ads with the knowledge that teens are always texting. This makes social media an even more important safe haven against unsolicited ads.

Marketing professionals are constantly sending messages to consumers, using every ploy to grab their attention and achieve their goals: sell, sell, sell! This can be counterproductive because unsolicited advertising may ultimately have a negative effect on a brand. This doesn't mean all advertising is bad—smart, appealing advertising can put a smile on anyone's face.

The best advertising is always a positive customer experience. I once wrote an article in the Dutch newspaper *Het Parool* about a winter offer from the UPC Cable Company, and said that it was true what they offered—their bad customer service would definitely leave you out in the cold. I had spent several hours on the phone with their customer service line, which nearly drove me to tears. But guess what? The new UPC has changed, and now I would even consider joining their Facebook page (if they had one) to let the world know that UPC listens and provides solutions. Brands can change their service and attitude!

Now, I read 50 stories a day online about how Twitter works as a targeted marketing tool, that a click through rate of seven percent can be achieved from a Facebook page, that Hunch.com is generating an algorithm for ads that targets subconscious brand preferences, and that Google will be able to index videos based on verbal content. There are so many exciting things happening online and every week new books are published full of insights and interesting theories about how marketing and (customer) service should be conducted today. I can imagine that you, as an entrepreneur or marketing manager, are being driven completely crazy by all these constant developments.

Of course, you know about web 2.0, and you send personalized emails to your customers, and you consider using Twitter, albeit under pressure from your colleagues and the media, and maybe you even have a cool iPhone application in the pipeline. But why do it? It's more work and possibly, in dispersing your message (and your budget), the target audience may not even be reached. I talk on an almost daily basis with marketing managers who are faced with difficult choices: "My media agency tells me that the media plan is good but I am doubtful..." They even say: "Social media is all hype and is only a passing fad..."

My advice is to listen to your gut feeling and common sense, not to the traditional media agency. They will always advise you to spend more money on more "reliable" and "trustworthy" (for them) media. Media agencies want the client to invest in media that they control, to justify their 15 percent commission. Here's the biggest change maker: you can save 50 percent or more on your current media budget. Stop sending information to large groups of people you don't know, hoping to find your target market among them. Switch the dial from broadcasting to a nonstop and open dialogue. Listen, ask, learn, and *then* sell. Your customers form the basis of your current success. Make them feel important and they will be your advertising channel.

A satisfied client can be your ambassador and "brand advocate." Instead of wasting valuable money and resources trying to garner unknown GRPs (Gross Rating Points), spend time getting to know and understand individual customers. The customer is more important, powerful, and assertive than ever, yet is still too often seen as part of the flock. Therefore, you need to start thinking and acting differently. "Think small, grow big" is a mindset and a plea to be conscious of the fact that today's consumers can share negative experiences concerning your organization online. Posts tainting your name will be forever locked away in the Google archive.

I thought long and hard about how many words I would write for the information that I want to share. Should I write a voluminous book, which only the die-hards would read completely? After meeting with Edward de Bono during IncrediblEurope in Vienna and reading his book *Six Thinking Hats*, I knew that *Think Small, Grow Big* would be something that could be read in one night. How much spare time do you have and how long do you want to spend to get to the core of social media?

So, this is not a dry list of facts, but a DIY book for a solid start with social media. Included is a concrete five-step plan and many tips, tricks, hints, and links to get going on this new path and significantly impact your company's growth. I hope everyone who loves communications and marketing—from strategists and trend watchers, Flash designers and copywriters, concept thinkers and PR consultants—will be happy to read this book. If you have any comments on what I have to say or want to get a discussion going about the topics presented in this book, you can email me at ab@juniorsenior.nl, direct message me on Twitter via @abkuijer, or mention the book in a tweet, blog post, or Facebook update with the hashtag #TSGB. In this way I will be able to respond quickly to your comments and thank you publicly for your support.

—Ab Kuijer, Nice/Amsterdam 2010

CHAPTER 1

THE HISTORY OF ADVERTISING, PART I

"When we change the way we communicate, we change society."
—Clay Shirky, Professor in New York University's
Interactive Telecommunications Program

courtesy of www.wikipedia.com

IMAGINE YOURSELF ON A DUSTY ROAD, THE Coliseum to your right, a public bath house to the left. Nailed to the entrance is a sign: "Public execution next week!" Or perhaps, "The Emperor's new club, unlimited food and drink!" These are certainly not the literal texts of fliers and posters of antiquity, but we do know that advertising is almost as old as the proverbial road to Rome. In Greek and Roman times, posters were hung to announce coming events. Ancient advertising also relied on word of mouth (passed along by those who could read) to ensure that the news continued to spread. This is recognized today as buzz marketing.

After the Middle Ages, literacy was by no means widespread and still presented a problem for advertisers, so logos were created to identify a business establishment. The tailor's logo was a suit, the blacksmith's, a horseshoe, and the barber's, a pair of scissors. The media landscape was flat and organized: the town crier shouted loudly (in return for a haircut) that the barber gave the best shaves around; walking billboards depicting a loaf of bread with an arrow made clear where the nearest bakery was located. Interestingly, these methods of advertising can still be seen on the streets of any major city or town. It used to be that advertising agencies did not exist. Eventually, though, new methods of advertising had to be introduced.

News organizations used to gather and disseminate news themselves. Only gradually did they start to sell advertising space within their pages. Pioneers in selling media space were Volney Palmer in the U.S. and Charles-Louis Havas in France. The honor of being the first full-service agency goes to N.W. Ayer and Son in Philadelphia, Pennsylvania, founded in 1869. They specialized entirely in the design, development, and placement of advertising messages. The original advertisements were generally newsworthy—any sort of artistic expression in print was, at the time, good reason to get noticed. Coca-Cola demonstrated this in 1920. The advertisement seen on the next page was just a simple (colorful) image, and for that reason alone consumers still read the brief message contained within. Communication was as simple as that.

courtesy of www.cocacola.com

New opportunities presented themselves with the advent of radio in the 1920s. Families used to gather around the radio, ears pricked, eagerly listening to the familiar voices of the presenters. The news and music programs were the most popular broadcasts, enjoyed by young and old alike.

During the intermissions, voice actors were used to present singing commercial messages. Depending on the budget of the advertiser, there could be as many as two, three, or four actors in a single advertisement. Soap was the most popular product advertised, followed by beer, soup, and cigarettes. There are still a number of wonderful examples of these advertisements available for listening online at www.oldtimeradiofans.com under the link "Old Radio Commercials."

courtesy of www.hearingvoices.com

While radio captured the imagination of the public, commercially deployable mass direct marketing also developed rapidly. The 1872 Montgomery Ward catalog, which featured no fewer than 163 products, made consumers feel special. All of the sudden shoppers were getting a whole store delivered to their doorsteps, giving the recipient a feeling of truly personal service.

courtesy of www.wikipedia.com

In 1935, Leo Burnett started an advertising agency, not knowing that his would become the fourth largest agency in America and the fifth largest in the world. Burnett was always in search of subconscious emotion. "You need the attention, otherwise there is no point advertising. But the trick is to stand in a natural way, without shouting or hogwash." Everyone wanted to work at Leo Burnett and young people constantly asked him how he had gotten into the world of advertising. His answer: "I am often asked how I got into the business. I didn't. The business got into me." Part of the reason the Leo Burnett Agency succeeded was because it knew how to advertise products with emotion. An exemplary example of this is one of Burnett's greatest and most loyal customers, the Marlboro Cowboy.

courtesy of www.leoburnett.com

Cigarettes are the best example of advertising a product with emotion. The content, color, and smell of a product are less important than the image being sold. Cigarette smoking at that time was associated with style, status, and considered conducive to social contact. To find a modern product that promises to make life more interesting and sociable, one need look no farther than the popular social networks. Facebook is the new online cigarette.

Another familiar name from this period is William Bernbach, co-founder of full service agency DDB and immortalized through his work for Volkswagen.

courtesy of www.ddb.com

The copy on the "Lemon" advertisement reads:

This Volkswagen missed the boat.

The chrome strip on the glove compartment is blemished and must be replaced. Chances are you wouldn't have noticed it; Inspector Kurt Kroner did. There are 3,389 men of our Wolfsburg factory with only one job: to inspect Volkswagens at each stage of production. (3,000 Volkswagens are produced daily; there are more inspectors than cars.)

Every shock absorber is tested (spot checking won't do), every windshield is scanned. VWs have been rejected for surface scratches barely visible to the eye.

Final inspection is really something! VW inspectors run each car off the line onto the Funktionsprüfstand (car test stand), tote up 189 check points, gun ahead to the automatic brake stand and say "no" to one VW out of fifty.

This preoccupation with detail means the VW lasts longer and requires less maintenance, by and large, than other cars. (It also
means a used VW depreciates less than any other car.)

We pluck the lemons; you get the plums.

Bernbach was an old-fashioned ad man with several "quotes" to his name—see how these have stood the test of time. Many advertising people can still identify with this fixed, one-way-forward thinking:

"Logic and over-analysis can immobilize and sterilize an idea. It's like love—the more you analyze it, the faster it disappears."

"Let us prove to the world that good taste, good art, and good writing can be good selling."

"All of us who professionally use the mass media are the shapers of society. We can vulgarize that society. We can brutalize it. Or we can help lift it onto a higher level."

"Nobody counts the number of ads you run; they just remember the impression you make."

"The truth isn't the truth until people believe you, and they can't believe you if they don't know what you're saying, and they can't know what you're saying if they don't listen to you, and they won't listen to you if you're not interesting, and you won't be interesting unless you say things imaginatively, originally, freshly."

"Good advertising builds sales. Great advertising builds factories."

"A principle isn't a principle until it costs you something."

"Rules are what the artist breaks; the memorable never emerged from a formula."

1949 Zenith 28T925R (USA) 10" Screen, "Mayflower"

© 2002 TVhistory.TV (Dunedin)

courtesy of www.history.tv

The First Television Commercials

In the 20th century, the media landscape was becoming more diverse. In addition to direct mailings and radio, newspaper, outdoor advertising, television advertising finally arrived in 1940. In England the belief was that television was designed to inform the public and no one should have been bothered with commercial messages. In America, the land of unlimited possibilities, the thought was very different. Television meant a captive audience; it had so much potential and could earn a company incredible money, so the view was, "let's use it!" In the 1950s, TV shows were sponsored by a brand or a specific industry: for instance, the "United States Steel Hour" sponsored drama on television from 1953-1963.

Other commercial television stations, such as the Dumont Television Network, also searched for major sponsors for their shows, though it was often easier said than done. To offset this, they decided to cut advertising airtime into 30-second chunks to make it more affordable for smaller advertisers. This idea was the forerunner to the format we know so well today. To sell a product in 30 seconds was a totally new concept that required a more innovative way of thinking. Television offered more opportunities to advertisers, but to convey emotions and create a new-style 30-second commercial required more than simply using a logo image and a smooth voice. Advertisers needed a concept, a film script, and essentially a new brand of communication. From this, the creative advertising agency was born. In the history of the American advertising industry, this period is known as the Creative Revolution.

The very first television commercials on the black and white picture tube were a sensation. America was the first on the scene in 1941, when the watchmaker Bulova suddenly came into view before the start of a baseball game and a voice spoke the famous words: "America runs on Bulova time." England followed much later; the first commercial on ITV was aired on September 22, 1955, for Gibbs S.R. toothpaste. In the Netherlands, the premiere T.V. commercial didn't air until January 2, 1967. Ironically, the advertiser was the Union for Newspapers, which promoted themselves as a more thorough media type than television.

AMERICA RUNS ON BULOVA TIME

courtesy of www.bulova.com

Television is still the medium that provides the greatest impact and range at the lowest cost. It is, however, a one-way broadcast channel, where a dialogue, despite "red button" experiments, is not possible. Nonetheless, from the sixties onward, economic outlook improved, production was increasingly automated, and we became a prosperous, consumer-driven society. Advertising was interesting, fun, and a normal part of our lives. We memorized the jingles and slogans, and we saw advertising as credible communication.

The Free Market in the Netherlands and Beyond

Despite their love for new forms of communication, consumers had little control over the content on official radio and TV stations, so they started free "pirate" channels to supplement official broadcasts with "unofficial" ones. In the Netherlands, radio stations like Caroline, Northsea, and Veronica became hugely popular, transmitting inland from their studios, equipped with transmitters and antennae located on "pirate ships" in the North Sea. In Amsterdam, the pirate TV channel Einstein showed erotic movies that could not be viewed on the official Netherlands One, and in more rural areas, you could listen to Radio Mexico playing non-stop Dutch songs. There are not many radio stations that play Dutch songs all day for good reason, but apparently there is an audience for everything!

courtesy of www.popupcity.net

In 1979, Amsterdam was shaken up with Weekend Radio Decibel (WRDB), which introduced a whole new way of making radio: very American, very fast, and with young, talented radio producers like Jeroen van Inkel, Daniel Dekker and John Holden (a.k.a. Adam Curry). The station catered to the needs of thousands of listeners and fans. Decibel still enjoys great popularity thanks to their success in the eighties.

courtesy of www.jr-sr.com

Politicians reacted slowly to the wave of civil dissatisfaction and the call for the establishment to change with the times. Eventually the popularity of the illegal stations was recognized, with Wave Amsterdam Power Sound (WAPS) becoming the first pirate radio station in the Netherlands to be awarded a license in 1985, the National Year for Youth.

A few years later, the possibility of privately-owned

commercial radio and television became a reality and the floodgates opened, offering a plethora of new radio and television stations. This was not only happening in the Netherlands, but all over Europe. Almost overnight, every country changed the media law and people were overwhelmed with hundreds of new TV channels and radio stations. The only problem was that there were still only 24 hours in the day!

For the advertiser, this sudden proliferation of television and radio stations posed many problems and things certainly became more confusing. Should an advertising budget be split over these different media as the target audience remained the same, but had no particular loyalty to any one medium, be it television or radio? With more channels and more ways to advertise, and the only way to get the message across to the consumer was to increase the frequency. Advertising expenditure rose to unprecedented levels, media agencies multiplied, and as advertising grew, the egos and salaries of the agency creatives and directors escalated to new heights.

The pressure on advertisers from media agencies to increase their media budgets meant more advertising revenue for the creative arm of the industry. Initially, the way things worked was simple: the marketing agency created a campaign and the advertiser bought it. In exchange for this, the cut for the agency was a 15 percent commission. This 15 percent fee was considered a payment for the creative work the agency had to deliver. But this was not enough for some and so the big players came up with a clever plan in the late 1980s—they decided to split up the advertising agency structure into a media purchasing agency and advertising agency to maximize revenues. The idea was that the media purchasing agency would act for multiple clients simultaneously and negotiate additional benefits for their clients, the advertisers.

Advertisers were forced to become more marketing savvy during this time as well, mainly to avoid increased costs from the agencies. Advertisers now had to work with media strategists and pay them a 15 percent commission fee, and then pay a separate invoice from the advertising agency for the creative work. But advice from large, international advertising agencies was, and is, often self-serving. Advertisers receive proposals from them that include blinking billboards at Triple-A locations and rounds of expensive commercials at prime time—things that are good both for the agencies' Gross Rating Points (GRPs) and for the media purchasing arms which negotiate deals with those prime locations and top networks. For advertisers interested in social media, dialogue marketing, and database building, or for those who simply want to listen to their customers, this type of marketing is expensive and unnecessary.

Without asking for social media or dialogue marketing, which the agencies have no vested interest in, the media budget goes down the drain quickly. For advertisers who do dare to ask for social media activation, the media agencies offer their in-house "interactive dialogue social media unit," which can also be used during the campaign period. This is not a good idea because a social media campaign is not a manually deployable tool. Social media is something natural; the content should come from your own organization and is in fact an ongoing live campaign.

I am deliberately overstating the situation and fortunately there are exceptions, but in my view, things went downhill when the agencies split the media arm from the creative. Where the original media planner and creative director liaised from day one, sat in on the same brainstorming sessions and worked hand-in-hand inside the same full-service advertising agency, now they are two separate entities that hardly interact. Today, the men and women who call themselves media planners are just boring accountants, wedged into a corner office where they produce pretty graphs and worry about the number of GRPs. Media planners became the "number crunchers" in a creative industry. I am sure they would like to be part of the creative campaign development again. And that is, in fact, where they belong. Money has taken over the logic of how creatives and planners should work together on the marketing action.

CHAPTER 2

IF YOU TELL IT, THEY WILL COME

"Social Networking that matters is helping people achieve their goals." —Seth Godin, Seth Godin's Blog

A S MORE AND MORE CHANNELS OF COMMUNI-cation open up, television is still the best media to invest in to quickly reach the masses. The difficulty lies in the number of commercials you need to broadcast to make a significant impact. But your commercial is not the only one people will watch. Creative agencies are using all their powers to get the message across: from special effects to space invasions, famous actors, cars, robots, and complete 3D animation films, no effort is spared to win an award given by the creative advertising industry. The result of all this eye-candy entertainment is that the packaging of a story became more important than the actual story, making it difficult for consumers to recall specific brands as a result. Trying to pin down the most impressive commercials and the brands associated with them can be tricky at best.

Using extreme gimmicks to impress the TV audience is not difficult to do. But the return on investment is comparatively low. How can advertisers expect the consumer to remember their message if the story is not actually from them, but made up by the creative media agencies? Brands should get back into storytelling. For example, Louis Vuitton had a wonderful commercial last summer that featured people who are traveling to famous cities around the world. The only text in the entire ad states, "Where will life take you? Louis Vuitton." Simple, but effective and true to the brand.

Consumers are always looking for a good story, something they can learn from the brand and about the brand. Consumers constantly ask, "What does it mean to me and why should I believe it?" Now is the time for advertisers to start telling more about themselves, why they do what they do and what makes them stand out from their competitors. Admittedly, this requires a whole new approach and a different briefing for the agency. But storytelling is going to be the biggest "new thing" for everyone working in the communications industry. The consumer is constantly exposed to creative nonsense and all they want is clarity, honesty, and above all, a good story. Wrapped in a pretty package, of course.

There are a few brands that, over the years, have sold their products with heart and soul and a clear message. They are now reaping the benefits. But what do you do when you're not Nike, Apple or Blackberry? Many marketing professionals are in a pickle: they grew up with a commitment to, and the ethos of, old media. They are well aware of the rules of the old economy. But Generation Y, the web 2.0 generation born between the years 1976–1995, and Generation Z, the "net generation" born between 1995–2009, ignore all rules and go their own way. They assume that advertising is fake and that brands are only friendly to sell more units. This is the clear language of the consumer of tomorrow. So what can you do to reach this new generation?

The best way to communicate with this generation and

help them connect is through a balance of traditional and social marketing. Many advertisers said goodbye to their strategic advertising agencies in favor of writing briefs for newer, hipper agencies in the hopes that they might stumble on the golden apple that would put their sales back on top. The pressure to deliver results was enormous, with advertisers clamoring for YouTube hits and front-page ads, delivered yesterday to their front doors. And if the viral videos and late-night events don't boost sales, it is not the advertiser's fault; they did everything they could. It is the fault of the stubborn consumer, the media that did not want to write about the product because it was too commercial, and the agency that didn't do its job. Advertisers are loathe to take responsibility for their own sales.

courtesy of Martyn Moore (mmoo on Flickr)

Short-term actions may attract attention, but without further follow-up, no value is added to a brand, and the efforts are ultimately a waste of time and money. It is proven that a good idea can attract attention, but do little to further sales and brand loyalty in the long term. For a good example of this, look at the Old Spice commercial in which former American football star Isaiah Mustafa tells viewers what Old Spice means to life as a man.

courtesy of www.youtube.com

Thanks to the clever commercial with the promise, "We're not saying this body wash will make your man smell like a romantic jet fighter pilot, but we are insinuating it," Old Spice attracted nearly ten million views on YouTube. The marketing manager is happy with sales figures, which indicates that the "don't-take-your-brand-too-seriously" strategy works. At the same time, competitors Nivea and Gillette achieved even better growth rates with coupons and traditional media support. Which advertiser is right?

Is Old Spice the winner because they are scoring online with a clear "pull" for the viral video that was viewed by the consumer of their own volition? Or are Nivea and Gillette the winners because they have performed and achieved results through more targeted marketing? The truth lies somewhere in the middle because, in general, the market for male grooming products has grown. And if a customer is looking for a nice new shower gel and everyone around is talking about Old Spice, why wouldn't they give it a try? In the case of Old Spice, sales boosted and the company got more customers, but not nearly with the same results as competitors using traditional marketing.

Often, direct marketing—a below-the-line technique tailored to target individuals—is viewed unfavorably by above-the-line media agencies that have much larger budgets for television commercials and can more easily establish brand recognition to a mass audience through creative and entertaining ads. But in the end, the ideal strategy for any company, large or small, should be a mix of viral and traditional marketing. Be effective by communicating with your audience using the same media they do to create direct sales. Then connect with them using social media. That's the start of a relationship and not a commercial flirt.

Direct marketing should be the basis of all communication with the customer. Advertisers should know their customers, customize offers to suit them, and open a dialogue with them. But too often the opposite is done. The reality is that unlimited creativity (and money) prevails, making advertising a form of entertainment for the masses. Everyone is vying for the consumer's attention. They have to, when they are surrounded by hundreds of other sensational commercials. And it's the personalization, the individual connection to fans that suffers. I don't understand it anymore—flying panty liners, dancing cars, guitar-playing llamas—advertising has essentially become farcical with one creative expression after another. Even faster, even whiter, even better, more efficient. Consumers look at it, they laugh, but they don't believe a word that is said. And the next generation won't even bother with that.

CHAPTER 3

CONSUMERS CAN'T GET NO SATISFACTION

"You will make mistakes. If you are sincere about helping the community, the authenticity will show and your mistakes will be forgiven." —Zia Yusuf, CEO of Streetline, Inc.

PEOPLE ARE GOING TO INCREASINGLY TURN AWAY from advertising when constantly faced with junk mail, fliers stuck in bike handlebars and car windows, dodgy salesmen ringing the doorbell, longer commercial breaks, text message ads, and cell phone cold calls. In Spain, a law was passed last summer that allows advertising for twelve minutes per hour on television. Now, that will help the ratings!

No wonder then, that the consumer's salvation is to be found on the Internet in sub-networks, looking for peers to communicate with in an advertising-free environment. Unfortunately, any social network that gets picked up by media agencies will suddenly become a happy hunting ground with Google AdSense banners that thrive based on the content posted or sites visited. The owner of the website will be thrilled that the site is generating advertising revenue, but the user will just be faced with more unsolicited advertising.

A humorous anecdote concerns the 13-year-old nephew of Rupert Murdoch, who was asked in early 2005 by the Board of Directors which media he and his classmates used. "Everyone is on MySpace, that's the place to be!" he told them. MySpace then was this hip, new online network where teens would hang out. Murdoch bought it immediately and pumped hundreds of millions of advertising banners into the site as if it were a traditional media channel. Within two years, MySpace was almost dead because the audience ran away, looking for another tribe, preferably one without all the ads. MySpace has managed to win back some ground thanks to its fair privacy policies and focus on music, but it still doesn't have near the audience it used to.

The mighty Proctor & Gamble, who has enriched lives with products like Head & Shoulders and Crest, opened an office next to Facebook in early 2010 so that the marketers could work together closely. But they were unsure how to deal with over 500 million users accessing their brand. They needed to fine-tune their advertising strategy to reach their target audience. I've been afraid of the plain actions and banners that we will soon be forced to watch. It is not unrealistic to think that a large group of Facebook users will soon look to an alternative network, free of unsolicited advertising, not unlike the MySpace situation.

Clay Shirky, a professor at New York University and the most famous blogger and writer on social media, said it eloquently: "New technology enables new kinds of group-forming." And it all happened so fast. So fast that we are still gasping for breath, causing outgoing Unilever boss Simon Clift to say that social media is hardly being understood by his own marketing managers. Clift, voted best marketing director in 2009, said in an interview with the *Financial Times* that his marketing people between the ages of 30 and 45 are "a lost generation."

> The group of marketers in the 25 to 30 age bracket knows from experience how digital media works and what it means to them. The group aged 45 and over knows this through their children and therefore only secondhand. The intermediate group, however, has to deal with phenomena and mechanisms with which they are not familiar. A lost generation. PR agencies understand it better than our own social media marketing employees. Unilever is invisible in social networks even though we provide many products for the consumer!

Things have started to change because the consumer now has web 2.0. The Internet is more interactive than ever and makes it easy to access important information that they can share with anyone and everyone. The Internet brings people out of their isolation and opens new doors in an extremely simple way. With a little effort and within a matter of weeks, one can acquire a few hundred new acquaintances that are prepared to share their photos and videos without reservation.

Consumers have also become more fascinated with the mobile Internet, downloading billions of apps and giving their opinions on uncensored websites like Zagat and Foursquare. The responsible consumers of today can now upload their opinions on the Internet to warn others or make recommendations. It is like flashing your headlights at drivers on the other side of the highway, warning them about the speed trap up ahead.

The consumers are all doing the same thing: it's the people against the rulers, united against the companies—the aggressive advertisers and traditional media with their bombardment of unsolicited advertising.

CHAPTER 4

WINNING OVER THE LITTLE GUY

"What's required is a kind of social media sherpa who can find you the audience you seek, who can reach out to them on the platforms where they are already congregating, and who can help promote in tasteful ways that fit the sensitivities of the networks where your audiences are found." —Chris Brogan, Author of Trust Agents

THROUGH SOCIAL MEDIA, THE MASSES TRY TO escape from unsolicited and annoying advertisements. Consumers prefer YouTube and Hulu to television and direct messaging to email.

This does not mean that no one is interested in advertising, promotions, or new product launches. On the contrary, advertising is good as long as it is communicated on a timely basis and made as personalized as possible.

"Think small, grow big" means that you as an entrepreneur, marketer, or communications expert need to start thinking like a consumer. Get out there and listen to your customer, whether it's your smallest, your biggest, or your first client. This means learning about the reliable customers, those who pay bills on time and have always been loyal, instead of focusing only on tough or difficult clients. It means knowing your entire customer base and working to satisfy everyone. Many marketing managers think that they know their customers well because they conduct marketing research each year. Yet that is not the same as talking to clients; it might give a random indication, but the individual relationship with your customers does not truly benefit from research and statistics.

Think of the small neighborhood grocer on the corner, who recognizes and personally greets his customers. It's good for the customer to be valued and be rewarded for repeat visits. "Hello Ab, how are you? I know you like your Chilean red wine and I've got a great offer just for you today!" I will not say no to such personal attention, especially when it is ultimately beneficial to me. Likewise, I want my shopkeeper to respect my privacy, not to be someone who pushes spam through my mailbox, knocking on my door every evening to ask if I would like to buy a bottle of wine. I don't need products that I know about or enjoy to be pushed in my face on a constant basis; I'll purchase a product or sign up for a service when I need or want it. Respect and loyalty is bi-directional, it works both ways.

Many people have an opinion about a company or product and know that they can put it on the Internet, for better or for worse. More than 20 percent of the 65 million daily tweets on Twitter are about a brand or a service. Add to that the fact that Twitter, in September 2010, was the third most popular search engine in the world after Google and YouTube, and it's obvious that many consumers seek brand information via Twitter. And the numbers continue to grow because consumer behavior patterns are changing. People prefer to express their views through web 2.0 and try brands based on word of mouth rather than advertising. It's almost as though we've harkened back to the old days of advertising, when the only way news about a product or service got around was through word of mouth!

When and how a business is talked about is becoming increasingly important. The website might be informative, the brochures full of powerful one-liners, and the TV commercial funny, but it is the digital credibility of a business that will make a difference. Having a strong virtual reputation is more important than achieving 300 GRPs or a printed circulation of one million. If the choice is between spending millions on reaching a mass audience without knowing who they are or spending a fraction of the cost on a small group of current customers, do the latter. It's smarter financially and will garner better long-term results.

Spending less money to focus on a smaller target audience is better than spending more money to gather a huge, wide-spread audience. It is the law of inverse numbers, which takes on more importance in these times when all the laws of media have been turned on their heads and why traditionally-thinking agencies have to rotate 180 degrees. The marketing manager or consultant who stubbornly continues to advise the use of traditional media "because it has worked so well in the past" is a dinosaur, a relic that cannot survive. I regularly meet with such people, and once I hear the insult, "You only think online," I know that I can demonstrate the best way to get to know existing customers and win new ones is through dialogue marketing, but they will opt for a dinosaur agency in the end.

I have a simple breakdown for your new media budget. Suppose you can reach one million people on paper with your current budget. That's a lot of customers, but realistically, maybe there are only 100,000 of those people who are actually interested in what you're selling and maybe 50,000 will remember your name and web address. Of those 50,000 people, 10,000 will take the time to look at the offer.

The first thing those 10,000 potential customers will do

is go online and look for reviews from other users who have already purchased the product. And they will always ask their friends whether the brand is reliable and a good value for the cost. With social media, consumers can reach more people and read brand reviews and customer experiences online. If the reviews are mostly negative, then the advertiser has a serious problem. Consumers are looking for the truth and will search for warnings from fellow customers. The service department, often the most neglected department within a company, may have forgotten a few disgruntled clients, or instructions from management may have limited the level of service on an offer. All too often, confused and angry customers get told that company policy limits the help they can receive and the consumer is left just as dissatisfied, if not more so, than before he placed the call. In the end, the company could have spent just a little extra time and money to win that customer over for life. Instead, with a traditional, straight-laced approach, they lose hundreds of potential customers through poor online reviews.

It's a fact that customers who are disappointed with the service of a company will vent their negative experience on the web. It's their only weapon, but a very powerful one. The Internet forgets nothing. Of those 10,000 people that will investigate an offer, you might lose 5,000 that are uncertain about your quality and service after reading some HR horror stories. And so when your fiscal year ends, you officially state that you've reached one million new people, but the truth is that you have no idea who they were (and you didn't actually get that many new customers). Meanwhile, other people are commenting about you online for all to see and your reputation is completely out of your hands. Media budgets could be spent much more efficiently; for example, to train marketing and customer service staff to work together in a more effective manner.

If knowledge about social networking and dialogue marketing is kept up to date, it will automatically dictate what is being communicated to the customer, and where the emphasis should be placed. Of course, we need mass media to get a message across and to create awareness. But the final battle for the customer is online.

CHAPTER 5

CREATING AMBASSADORS

*"Quit counting fans, followers and blog subscribers like bottle caps.
Think instead about what you're hoping to achieve with and through
the community that actually cares about what you're doing."*
—Amber Naslund, Social Media Today

MAKE A 180 DEGREE TURN IN THE WAY YOU think. Activate your basic network of shareholders, employees, suppliers, and existing customers and make them ambassadors. Write your mission statement, the story about the creation of your firm, and make it clear why you feel that, for example, you make the best car in the world. Go full throttle with your enthusiasm and share your knowledge. Collect fans and pay attention to them. Then provide them with special digital content that they can easily and voluntarily forward to their friends on your behalf. Organize simple promotions (retweet this item and every day someone wins), launch small online quizzes, play games with a great chance to win something, send a viral video to your base network, spread interesting and fun content about the company and join the discussions that arise thereafter. Share your brand with your ambassadors; you can learn a lot from them.

Make sure that you include your message on every major social media channel. Adidas advertising in soccer stadiums does not read `adidas.com` anymore but `www.facebook.com/adidasfootball`. Adidas marketeers are playing it smart; they understand that consumers are using their Facebook page. One click and they connect with the Adidas brand. And their friends on Facebook see this and think, "Oh yes, Adidas, that's a brand I want in my network, too."

Reward everyone who joins your Facebook page with a discount voucher when they register that they can then use at their local store. Send them a message after registration with a link to a digital gadget they can download for free. There are dozens of strategies that you can use to expand your fan base.

On average, Facebook users have 160 friends, so having 1,000 people in your direct network can activate another 160,000 people, which in return activates their networks. The bottom line is, with 1,000 people in your immediate network, you can quickly reach the same one million consumers you reached with expensive mass media. But now these people have received your message through their friends and acquaintances, which is a stronger, more effective way to get your messages to the audience! Now you have a growing number of people who are aware of your brand and there is a growing appreciation of and empathy for your company. The next step is to find a logical way to be part of a social network. The key word here is dialogue. Stop traditional one-way thinking, stop sending commercial messages and go listen to the receiver. What do they actually want?

One thing you can do for your new fans is place a link to a secret video that will be officially released in three weeks' time. Chances are that the link will be redirected, and this will increase the buzz around your brand or product. Be creative and make the target audience feel they are part of the buzz; they are after all, the ambassadors of your brand.

It is crucial to give plenty of advance notice about specific product launches and other important matters through your social media channels. The diagram below from social media outfit MediaSnackers shows how the so-called "tipping point" is clear—at some point your audience will generate more content and news than you've put forward.

If you have a product launch or a special sales promotion on the agenda, start today with your pitch—the whys and wherefores, the preparations, photos, videos, the people behind the scenes.

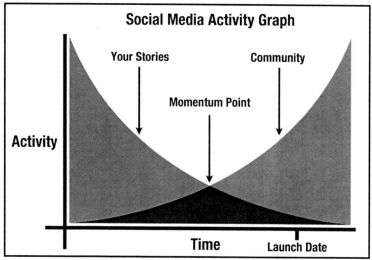

Social Media Activity Graph

On the momentum point illustrated in the above graph, it can be seen how information is picked up and forwarded to others. In the upward trend when the community is supporting you, you formally introduce your product.

By marketing your brand through a social network, you

can portray it as fun, inspirational, and emotional. Make sure the information provided is relevant and the context is immediately clear. You should also provide additional useful product information for your current customers. You're here to communicate with your audience in a way that seems revolutionary, but is in fact as old as the hills. Only now, the road there requires a different knowledge and understanding of the new media landscape.

CHAPTER 6

TWITTER 101

"Tweets are the gold standard of scoops. A growing number of newspapers are turning their entire mastheads over to Twitter."
—*Woody Lewis, Social Media Advisor to News Organizations.*

TWITTER IS THE THIRD MOST POPULAR SEARCH engine in the world after Google and YouTube, and each day more than 90 million tweets are posted. Twenty-five percent of all these posts relate to a company or product, including complaints and praise from consumers. This makes Twitter a good outlet for the frustrated user, but be cautious, if one wolf starts to howl, many others will do the same thing without thinking.

Air Canada found this out the hard way when they unfortunately damaged the specially-adapted wheelchair of a seriously ill boy who was en route to a well-known amusement park. Out of frustration, a message was posted on Twitter and within no time at all, Air Canada was being branded as a heartless enterprise with lack-luster customer service. In reality, they were trying to get the wheelchair repaired and had been doing so for two days—they had no idea news could spread so quickly and they could become so demonized in the virtual world. They finally employed a marketing executive who stemmed the tide of negative messages and launched a charm offensive whereby the wheelchair and the boy were taken to additional amusement parks as a gesture of goodwill.

An advertiser can actually do two things: ignore Twitter because there will always be those who will criticize, or realize that their "virtual reputation" is important. A negative virtual reputation can harm a company's image and sales. The saying that "all publicity is good publicity" would be what an old-fashioned PR expert might believe, but that is nonsense. Unfortunately, there are too many examples where an inadequate response to negative online buzz caused irreparable damage, not only in terms of the brand, but to turnover. Do a Google search for "United Airlines and broken guitar," or "Domino's Pizza and spit on the pizza." These are two classic examples that demonstrate the power of social media and have been rehashed dozens of times in books and extensively discussed and analyzed. You don't want to be that brand.

courtesy of www.tweetdeck.com

Damage to your virtual reputation can be easily avoided by setting up Tweetdeck (`tweetdeck.com`) to scan for references (@ mentions) about your company, so you can promptly respond to serious cases of negative customer experiences and set the record straight. An easy way to manage this is to give your customer service employees a Smartphone with Tweetdeck mobile and instigate a plan to constantly monitor the virtual world.

Using Hashtags in Twitter

Companies can use Twitter to post updates, called "tweets," about their services, customers, and products. It's a great free network and by using specific search words tied to a hashtag (#) inside the tweets, that tweet is immediately indexed with the hashtag in the Twitter search engine. The hashtag is a clever invention of Twitter; use it with your company name and special offers or events to maximize the benefit to your organization (e.g. If General Motors was having an Apple iPod giveaway, they could use the hashtag #gmipodpromo2011).

You can also automatically post tweets that link to blog posts with the use of "posting sites" such as Posterous.com or Ping. fm. Any status update on one of these sites will be automatically posted to Twitter, and any other site you want it linked to (including Facebook, your blog, your website, Digg, Reddit, etc.). When posting blog updates to Twitter, it is important that your post headlines are interesting and fit within the allotted 140 character limit, including space for a link to the article. If your link URL is too long, you can shrink it with `www.tinyurl.com`. By using capital letters in the heading, as with a newspaper headline, Google will notice the posts faster. Finally, feedback on specific posts from followers can be found through "Direct Messages" and "@ Replies." This can all be done through your Twitter page, but it is easier still with Tweetdeck.

"What can I do with Twitter? It doesn't seem very interesting!" I frequently hear these kinds of complaints during lectures, but really, it can be a beneficial tool for every entrepreneur. You need only to try it and see. One solution for making Twitter more manageable, especially for a business, is to invest a few bucks in special software such as Tweet Adder (www.tweetadder.com). This allows you to search within the millions of tweets per day for specific words in any language.

Imagine that you are a photographer and you search for tweets that might help you with your business or that have to do with photography. You might find questions like, "I am looking for an affordable photographer for a shoot tomorrow—anyone have a tip?" posted by someone in the online community. You could then respond with an offer: "Hello, look at my website, niceshot.com, and yes, I'm available tomorrow!"

Twitter is ideally suited to find sales leads. It is not the place to peddle your product. You don't go door to door asking if people need their vacuum cleaner fixed. But if you see a sign hanging on the door, "Vacuum cleaner repair needed!" then you should approach since you know someone is in need of your services.

Look for keywords that relate to your service or area of expertise. If you see, "I'm hungry!" tweeted in your area and you own a pizzeria, send an @ reply to the hungry person and offer a complimentary bottle of wine with every three pizzas purchased that night. Place the offer on Twitter and all your other channels: "Whoever retweets this message gets a bottle of wine with every 3 pizzas ordered until midnight." Before you know it, your restaurant is crowded with hungry people from a digital world. In the end, it's a hip, effective, and fun way to draw attention to your business.

You could also use a hashtag followed by a code word to launch a promotion for your followers and fans. Moonfruit, a hosting and web design business, was one of the first companies to launch a retweet contest. Anyone was invited to retweet clever phrases using the hashtag #moonfruit to be entered daily into a contest to win one of ten MacBooks in ten days to celebrate Moonfruit's tenth anniversary. It was mysterious (what was moon fruit?), and if you repeated the word, did you really stand a chance of winning a MacBook? What was there to lose? Moonfruit is now regarded as one of the most viral Twitter promotions on the Internet, and the company grew to its peak in July 2009 (the month of the contest), from 400 to more than 40,000 followers. That number has since halved as no follow-up strategy was employed—talk about a missed opportunity!

What we can learn from Moonfruit is that it is easy to create a contest and reward those who retweet your hashtag. Make sure that you follow up on your promotion. Keep your Twitter channel up to date with worthwhile content. That way you keep your followers and build a relationship with them. Invite them to an upcoming event or your Facebook page. Twitter can be a valuable tool when utilized properly. It can draw attention to your brand through the use of simple marketing techniques and build a following quickly and easily. It is a social network that seems designed to help the marketer and salesmen find ready-made fans for their products and services. Used wisely, it can make all the difference in the world of social marketing.

CHAPTER 7

FACING FACEBOOK

"A marketing person should always ask one key question when beginning to develop a social media strategy: how much chaos can this organization handle?" —Gary Stein, Vice President of Strategy for Isobar

IT IS INTERESTING TO WATCH AND PREDICT what Facebook will become. With more than 650 million users in 2011 and expecting *one billion* (!) users in 2012, including your grandma and that weird neighbor across the street, it has become a social network for everyone. It is impressive the impact Facebook can have on your brand, and you do not need to be Nike or Absolut Vodka to see the effect. Whether you're selling woodworking machinery in the Netherlands or a treatment plant in South America, the business market has become important to Facebook. This is largely because there are so many people on Facebook and the search engine is used frequently. If someone does a Facebook search about your company or products, they should be able to find you there!

For companies, there are two free options—to have a dedicated Facebook page or Facebook group. The most logical approach is to create a page for your business so everyone on Facebook can view your content. You can set up your page in such a way that your tweets are automatically posted to the page's wall, just as with your blogs and LinkedIn profile. The biggest downside to starting and running a Facebook page is that it must be linked to a personal profile; it cannot stand alone. If you open a group, you are effectively choosing to remain closed to a large part of the (Facebook) world, since people must request to join. In addition, you and your group "friends" can only have internal discussions, and the topics should remain relevant to the group. It's difficult to gather new fans with this option. The advantage of a group is that you can send messages to everybody in the group, a service that cannot be used for the fans who signed up for your Facebook page.

I recommend using a page that you promote as much as possible. Advertise your Facebook page on your business cards, your shop window, your price tags, and especially on your website. You should utilize the "Like" button for every article or page on your website. Ten minutes of work for your webmaster can produce great results: now a visitor to your site can indicate how much they like the content. With one click, they are redirected to your Facebook page. Another click can be the beginning of an online friendship. In addition, now you have a lot more information about your fans at your fingertips. These people may well be all your customers who want to become ambassadors. Thank them publicly on your wall and tweet their name with a hashtag before it.

It's important that you update your Facebook page at least once a week, providing something new for your followers, even if it's only a photograph or a link. Give people the chance to learn more about your business and the drive of the people behind the logo. Companies will keep very loyal customers if they dare to show emotion and genuine interest in other people.

Customers that buy from you only because of your low pricing strategy might next week visit your competitor who is happy with a smaller margin and offers a lower price. By paying attention to your customers, you add the most valuable service there is, and that will make a little price difference less important.

Below are some examples of photo content that you can post on your Facebook page:

- A line of people in your store (text accompanying photo: "Good results from our offer of the week!")
- The fleet of company cars getting washed (text accompanying photo: "You can only make one first impression on the customers.")
- Delivery of a nice cake at a party (text accompanying photo: "We have something to celebrate: a new client!")

You get the idea. You can even work on these months in advance with some stock photos. Once you have a sense of how

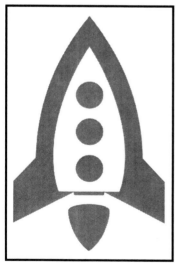

courtesy of www.jr-sr.com

to tackle it and feel confident about your editorial control, you can play with the actual news about your company and its activities. But always remember that anyone can see this information, including the competition!

If you have more than 25 fans on your Facebook page, you can register your company name as a Facebook name. This is important because companies are increasingly referring to their place in a social network instead of their own site. Learn from Adidas (www.facebook.com/adidasfootball) and protect your company name. For me, `www.facebook.com/ JuniorSeniorAmsterdam` is more important than the corporate website in the long run.

Facebook Promotions

The people who join your Facebook page have chosen to do so consciously; they are "friends" that like you, your brand, or your service. For these people, it is okay, even welcome, if you run a promotion on Facebook once a week and allow them to pass it on to their friends. Give them an additional discount, for example a code for ordering something online or a link to a voucher that can be printed off. Make some special offers just for Facebook. If others want to use this, they have to "Like" your page as well.

A free ticket to an event, a 50 percent discount on a workshop for the first ten Facebook fans that subscribe, these are the things that make the difference between an active Facebook page and a boring one. For creative agencies, Facebook is the ultimate medium. You can save on traditional media costs and hire the best creative people in the media who understand this. Your new promotional vehicle is out there and it's free.

courtesy of `www.facebook.com`

An example of one of the smartest Facebook campaigns is that of IKEA, made by the Swedish agency Forsman & Bodenfors. They used the "photo-tagging" feature to allow fans to connect their name with a picture and even the spot where their name would be placed.

For the opening of their new store in Malmö, Sweden, IKEA decided that the branch manager, Gordon Gustavsson, should create an account on Facebook. He said that he was proud of their showroom, and an operation was devised: the person who tagged their name on a product first in the photograph of the showroom became the owner of the chosen "tagged" product. Within days, the strength of a clear social network was evident, with hundreds of people visiting the IKEA page. A total of 25 photos of showrooms were posted and tens of thousands joined in on the action. It was a great success with minimal investments. You can watch the video for the event on YouTube; search for "brandcase + IKEA + Facebook."

Companies should ideally use their Facebook pages on a daily basis, and always have them open so they can respond to a question. In addition, they need to ensure that the right person is authorized to respond to these queries. Nestlé made the classic mistake of leaving a trainee in charge of their Facebook page. This led to embarrassing situations that ultimately damaged the reputation of the Nestlé virtual brand.

The administrator of the Facebook page forbade the use of the Nestlé logo as a profile picture. Anyone using it was told, "The logo is ours and if you persist in using it, you will be removed from this page." Yikes! How cool is it if one of your customers wants to walk around with your brand name on his or her forehead? That should be encouraged rather than prohibited. Greenpeace then opened a discussion on the page with questions concerning the use of palm oil in Nestlé products. The first reaction from the moderator was along the lines of, "Do not post questions such as this, this page is ours." Unfortunately, that's not how things work in a digital democracy.

When active online, you need to take into account the rules that exist where transparency, fairness, and dialogue are the marketing approaches of choice for companies who want to retain their customers and keep them enthusiastic about their brand. Show your clients that they matter to you. Show that you are prepared to take them seriously and deal with their queries on an individual basis. Think small, grow big.

While the Nestlé shareholders in Geneva smoked cigars and talked big deals, their reputation on Facebook went up in smoke. If they had realized how powerful the online consumer is, they might have had a more professional approach to their Facebook page from the outset.

Your Facebook page is not something to be trusted to your intern, but is a serious tool for your service and marketing department. When used appropriately, as with other social marketing tools, it can yield big results with just a little effort.

CHAPTER 8

CONNECTING WITH LINKEDIN

"Today people don't trust companies. One of the things marketers want to do is to humanize their brand. What better way to do it than put a live person in front of them?" —Jackie Huba, Author

courtesy of www.linkedin.com

L INKEDIN IS ONE OF THE STRONGEST NETWORKS for the business-to-business market. The range is very specific: 71 percent of the online world will never use it. Those who do use it are entrepreneurs or working at management level. Dutchman Perry van Beek is working as a LinkedIn coach (nl.linkedin.com/in/perryvanbeek); I am sure he never could have imagined doing a job like that ten years ago. Perry now has a full-time day job training people how to use

LinkedIn advantageously to boost their careers, generate leads, or build a good virtual reputation.

Note that LinkedIn is primarily a professional network. Having a clear profile is the first step in using LinkedIn effectively. The system works much like an online resume—you input professional information about yourself, such as what training you have received and where you work. It is important to make sure you optimize the engine power of LinkedIn: if your profile is 100 percent complete, you will rank highly with Google. For that reason only, you should not miss the opportunity to complete your LinkedIn profile; it is likely that before or after a personal meeting or interview, people will search your name to see what information is available about you.

One great networking aspect of LinkedIn is that it allows users to enter the address of their website under the "My Website" section on their profile page. They can also enter site details under "My Blog" and "My Company," adding up to three external URLs. Under the horizontal menu choices, there is an option to change the category "My Website" into "Other." If an individual doesn't have a webpage, they can enter a keyword, such as their specialty or name of their company or product and use LinkedIn-Google synergy to link this keyword to their name. Success guaranteed!

LinkedIn is, unlike most social networks, very suitable for hard selling. If your profile indicates that you are interested in business deals, you are assured that interested persons will take a direct approach. A professional business subscription costs several hundred dollars per year, but in exchange, subscribers get access to a wide selection of names and companies that may be useful contacts and future customers. LinkedIn is good for more than gathering contacts, too. Through its own email system, InMail, you get a response nine times out of ten. Such is the etiquette on LinkedIn; what goes around comes around.

To optimize your LinkedIn profile, make sure that it is up to date with current information and place the business content that you send out through your weekly blog as a status update via an RSS feed. You could also add your LinkedIn account to Ping.fm or Posterous.com, as with Twitter, Facebook, and blogs. With one click, your information is everywhere, including on your LinkedIn profile.

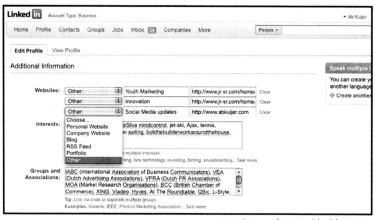

courtesy of www.abkuijer.com

Generating Leads in LinkedIn

LinkedIn is an ideal search engine with which to find new leads. Would you like to work for Sony Ericsson Europe, or are you looking for the regional manager of MEXX? Chances are an application for open positions or the manager can be found on LinkedIn. To connect with them, do not send a request asking them to join your LinkedIn network, but take a more subtle approach. Find out which groups they are members of, become a member of these groups yourself, and follow your prospect each week. Find out which discussions are of interest to them and where you can connect with them. By being members of the same groups and joining in the same discussions, you should be able to ensure that a connection does occur. As soon as it does, you can invite them to your LinkedIn network.

For each discipline there is a discussion group. From "the effective use of e-mail marketing" to discussions about "POS recyclable materials," LinkedIn provides a wealth of material and experiences and the opportunity for all to discuss, share, and learn from each other. If your specialist field is not listed, you can start your own group and initiate a new weekly discussion to engage potential customers. Discussing items and ideas of interest is an ideal way to attract new customers, rather than just by discussing price.

Good salespeople know that they can only sell when there is a trust relationship between customer and vendor. Through LinkedIn, you can build trust by regularly participating in subject-specific discussions. Deliver comments and share tips and solutions that show your expertise and understanding of the business. Over time you will be invited to join other discussion groups because they recognize your qualities. That way, you will steadily build your virtual reputation.

First-time customers looking to do business with a company will always ask for references. You can give out a list of companies you've worked for, but it is best if the responsible manager at Company X has a positive story to tell about their experience with you. On LinkedIn, customers and co-workers can give recommendations that will be displayed on your profile. While it might feel awkward asking former clients for recommendations and praise, it is a great way of finding out whether your customers are happy. If so, you have an additional sales tool in your hands, ready to be used. Recommendations are the fruits of recognition. Use them where you can further the profile of your company and that of yourself as a manager. New customers will certainly search your name on Google and read about you on LinkedIn. You want to ensure that, as someone they are about to work with, they will find you to be reliable and worthy of their business.

It is because of LinkedIn's incomparable business networking qualities that it should be in the online repertoire of every marketer and advertiser. It gives working professionals the ability to post all their professional skills and contacts quickly and easily, negotiate sales, and make and request recommendations. This makes LinkedIn a necessary tool for marketers who want to gather new and old customers into their circle, and should be added to the list of essential online networks along with Twitter and Facebook. With these three base networks, along with one more invaluable online tool, marketers and advertisers can accomplish online what they've been trying to do via traditional marketing for almost twenty years: know their customers.

CHAPTER 9

THE IMPORTANCE OF BEING AN EARNEST BLOGGER

"Blogging is a communications mechanism handed to us by the long tail of the Internet." —*Tom Foremski,* Silicon Valley Watcher

WEBSITES ARE HANDY FOR GATHERING a lot of information in one spot. You can have everything in one place—text, photos, blogs, videos, a shop, an intranet, and even a connection to your inventory system. All digital content is easily maintained with an open-source CMS system like Typo3, Joomla, or Drupal.

At JuniorSenior, we have produced many of these types of websites, but it is not enough today to ensure that a website can be found. With more than one billion websites in existence, it is increasingly difficult to attract new visitors to a website unless the URL is strongly promoted using AdWords, AdSense, link buying, link sharing, and email marketing. That is why I often say "no" if a client wants a site without having a digital strategy and vision in place. I explain to them that a search engine crawls the new website in the first week with a "spider" that indexes content. One week later, the spider returns to the website to check for new updates. If there is nothing new on the homepage, the spider won't check for new content for a month, instead of again in a week. The more content you post and the more frequently you post it, the more often your site will be indexed. In a month, if there is still nothing new content-wise, your website will move down the list again, and will only be indexed once a year. Instead of topping search engine results, your site is listed toward the end, pages behind other sites that update content at least once a week.

Using Keywords as Digital Magnets

In order to do better, consider creating digital magnets for your corporate website. This gives prospective customers another reason to search your website. Formulate five main everyday problems customers have that your business has a solution for, and then blog about these topics. Give each type of product or service a number of "tags" on your website. These are the main keywords that people will use to search for your products. Think as your client would when looking for a product—which search words do they use most? Gather the opinions of colleagues to help establish the best tags to use. Use these tags at least three times per 200 words in a blog post. This will ensure that your post will come up when a client searches online using your keyword phrase. For example, if your company sells tools, the keywords for power drills might be: power drill, online tools, tool kits, power tools, drill bits, drill sets, power drill kits, and so on. Anyone who searches for power drills online using those keywords should wind up at any site or blog posts indexed with those tags.

When writing a blog post, it does not really need to be longer than 200 words; people generally do not read long pieces of text on the Internet. If you have a longer story to tell, it is better to make a video. Open several blog accounts on free sites like blog.com, tumblr.com, wordpress.com, or blogger.com. Blogging does require discipline and must contain enough variety to continually appeal to your loyal readers and fans. The main reason I advise companies to blog is because it helps them create news value and increase their findability in the search engines. If you do not have time to do your own updates, hire a digital copywriter with sufficient knowledge of Search Engine Optimization (SEO) to update for you in a vivid and compelling way to appeal to your readership.

Suppose you own a transportation company involved in the leasing, maintenance, and security of trailers. You could open a separate blog for each service, for example, "Roadside Problems for Professional Drivers." Every week you write a story based on your experiences, interspersed with the chosen tag and a link for your followers directly to your website. Any link to a page within your site is called a "deep-link" and is valued more by Google. Even your next posts on "Roadside Problems for Professional Drivers" will deal only with relevant content for this audience (professional drivers who presumably encounter roadside problems). Within 48 hours you'll see that the blog search engine result is ranked higher than your own corporate site when people search for your subject matter or company. Why? Because a blog is always up to date with new content and Google likes this.

A blog can also be posted on your corporate site to reinforce its validity. Google will always have a preference for blogs as long as they are being continuously updated. Wordpress is the strongest blog hosting site in terms of indexing, and as such, more and more sites are being created as blogs in Wordpress to have the appearance of a normal website. In this way, all the content, stories, videos, and pictures are indexed by search engines.

Even if you use a Wordpress site, having extra digital channels with specific content is important for the findability of your business. Spread your story through as many channels as possible, especially where you know your target audience is. And if you do not know where they are, find them! Explore the online hangouts and habits of your target audience. It is better still if your blog is supported by sites that link back to it. You should already be doing this from your corporate site, but the more the merrier; create links from other blogs you may launch.

I hear you thinking: "I really do not have the time to do this!" Calculate how much money you spend on "unnatural" search engine optimization. It may well add up to a few thousand dollars per month. For that amount of money, you could have a smart social media person with journalistic ambitions employed in-house who will power up your position in the search engine with a well-written blog. No matter which approach you take—doing the work yourself or hiring an expert—remember that the time and money you spend now on natural SEO and blog development will pay off tenfold in the end, and the results will be better than if you had stuck with traditional marketing methods.

CHAPTER 10

GOING VIRAL

"If the Internet can be described as a giant human consciousness,
then viral marketing is the illusion of free will."
—*George Pendle, Journalist and Author,* `www.georgependle.com`

THE ROYAL DUTCH KLM AIRLINES PROMOTION
to win a free seat to New York, created by the Amsterdam
Lost Boys, was one of the first big online successes. The concept
was simple: you got an email from a friend with a link to the
promotional game. You had one chance to click on a seat. If you
chose the right seat, you won a ticket to New York. Of course I
never won anything, but I was able to try it again and again, and
each time I successfully invited three friends to participate by
email. The game was played millions of times and within a few
weeks KLM and New York were the talk of the town.

courtesy of www.jr-sr.com

courtesy of www.jr-sr.com

People love simple and fun activities and free games, and as long as your product is central to these activities, it is a great way to generate publicity. But do not expect miracles in terms of direct marketing unless the rules specifically require that a product and code must be purchased to participate.

My agency JuniorSenior created a 3D Flash game for Doritos in 2007. The rules were simple—participants got one game play for each code they had, one for each bag of Doritos purchased. The game involved a granny on a scooter with a basket. She was under a big tree where there were a variety of apples with different point values. By combining different options, such as two green apples, three red, one yellow followed by red, you got extra power for the electric scooter or a larger basket. These tips and tricks were hidden in the game rules (all 94 pages!) that we had posted anonymously on a gamers' site.

Within a week the first winners were published on the site. It was scheduled to take two weeks for the prizes (Apple laptops) to be delivered and the winners started complaining after a week that they had not received any prizes and the whole thing was a scam. Through online monitoring from day one, we were able to respond to these complaints immediately. Using blogs and forums we said that the rules clearly stipulated that it would be two weeks before the prizes arrived. A few days later there were positive posts on the website that the prizes had come and the news spread like wildfire. Within eight weeks more than 3.2 million people had played the game. For Doritos, that meant more than 3.2 million bags of chips were sold in eight weeks. They were one happy client.

courtesy of www.abkuijer.com

As a brand marketer, you can also pick up on the viral successes of others. On the photo sharing website Flickr.com, a girl started to photograph the contents of her handbag. This became more and more popular and in no time there was a group of approximately 10,000 photographed handbags. Moleskine, the Italian slim pocket diary manufacturer, picked up on this idea, started a Facebook page, and called on people to photograph the contents of their bags. The project was easily done and got Moleskine more than 52,000 fans as a result.

Of course, you can also ask your creative agency to do something memorable, but why reinvent the wheel when the potential is right in front of you to attract more fans that fit perfectly within your target group?

My advice is, if your idea fits in with existing viral successes, use it. Assume you sell a product that belongs in a handbag—lipstick, for instance. Search for crowded online hangouts where they talk about fashion, entertainment, or style and then post some nice messages about lifestyle and general entertainment. Join the conversation and activate a new user profile on the site.

The employee who manages the avatar will never talk about your commercial promotion. People on social networks do not need, want, or ask for advertising. Do make sure, though, that your avatar's account name and photo have a relationship with your business. In the case of your lipstick company, your online identity might be "Miss HighGloss." If you were to focus instead on men and own a car outlet center, your avatar could be "Mad Mustang Murdoch," who in real life works at a Ford Garage in Anytown, USA. The point is to choose a prominent profile that will be memorable. Man is curious by nature. Who is "The Beautiful Flower Girl?" After clicking on her profile, they discover that she has a flower shop. And on her homepage they see the message that Facebook fans get additional discounts when they order online. Any avatar profile that will grab attention and bring users back to your site or blog is worth using.

Actively participating in discussions that affect product and increase visibility online requires marketing professionals to combine normal human behavior and creativity. Consider the Internet as a main street where all groups of people are talking. Be polite, interested, and give away something nice; before you know it, you have some new friends. But again, do not actively peddle what you do. In your profile, you can obviously highlight what you sell. People will find out for themselves if they are interested. You can offer them something to buy, but only if they ask for it!

CHAPTER 11

MEASURING UP

"Actions speak louder than words. Businesses must act. Once the door to social consciousness is opened, bring the spirit of your company through it to affect change." —Brian Solis, Author of Engage *and Blogger at* `www.briansolis.com`

A LL THE HYPE ABOUT SOCIAL MEDIA AND the uncertainty of its return on investment is grist to the mill of the slow rotating media agencies. Marketers often get sour comments like, "It's nice, but honestly, what do you really get back?" and "With a TV commercial, at least you know how big your range is." Putting together a new media strategy is not an "and/or" choice, but a matter of effectively using the best of both worlds.

There are those who like to read the newspaper to keep updated with current affairs and those who rely on television news to inform them. Enticing these people to buy your product takes time and a lot of media pressure. Your current customers are increasingly active online and new generations have all grown up with web 2.0. They expect the same from you.

Your online audience will search for information about your product and rely more on the recommendations of their peers. They expect to find your brand in their virtual world just as it is in the real world. If your virtual acte de presence is good, then they might decide to become fans of your Facebook page and recommend your product to their friends. They might also be open to an invitation to spend a pleasant afternoon with you for a small presentation. But before integrating "think small, grow big" into your strategy, companies must invest in social media, or at least reorganize their media budgets. In going down this route, they must realize that it is a commitment to a new, open, honest way of communicating.

Zero-measurement

Obviously you want to look back on any social media investments and see that you have accomplished what you set out to achieve: a growing number of customers, a better image of your company, and ultimately more sales. The owners of the company want to see results, so you have to show stats. How do you deliver these?

Make a chart to impress the Board or owner. Start with a zero-measurement of your Facebook page, YouTube channel, Twitter account, and LinkedIn profile. Note how much money you currently spend on new customer acquisition. Also note the current page rank of your website on Google Analytics, your media budget, and which sorts of media you can measure in terms of response, including new prospects and new customers. Chart all measurable data that can be influenced by social media.

Include in your presentation what you know about your customers. That could prove disappointing at first, as customer databases are not always kept up to date. Sales statistics are hard figures, but the data relating to the people who contribute to these figures is still vague. Data mining can be like gold mining if you have more than just a name to put on top of the invoice. Enhance your database with information that enables you to better communicate with your customers directly. Record addresses, Skype names, birthdays, and social networks they belong to. The more you know about your customers, the better service you can provide. All customers, regardless of income or spending habits, are important.

If your marketing team doesn't have enough information about your customers, start to enrich your database with information from your sales team, or by organizing a survey using a Personal URL, the so called Purl (see Chapter 12, "Dialogue Marketing"). Show more interest in your customer! Ask how they like to receive information from you: by mail, email, phone, SMS, or Facebook. Find out which social media networks they know (MySpace, Facebook, Twitter, LinkedIn) and which networks they belong to.

Once you collect this information, the real work begins. As inspiration, here is an interesting case study from the March 2010 *Harvard Business Review Magazine.*[1] The question posed by the research team was, "How effective is a Facebook page for sales and customer loyalty?" A wonderful aspect of social networking to focus on as there are already so many theoretical books on human behavior vs. social networks; what we want is a real example of revenue improvement!

courtesy of www.abkuijer.com

Dessert Gallery (DG), a popular bakery and café chain in Houston, Texas, took part in such an experiment. A survey was sent out via email to 13,270 customers from the DG mailing list to find out about their buying habits and whether they were active online. Only 689 people responded; a fraction of the recipients, but a logical number, given that in today's life we get an enormous amount of email, much of it spam. A tasty Dessert Gallery Facebook page was started and anyone on the mailing list was invited to become a fan. The Dessert Gallery Page was updated several times a week with pictures of goodies, news about contests and promotions, links to rave reviews, and blog entries from DG employees.

Three months and 1,067 comments later, the first results were noted. A second survey was sent and recipients were divided into three groups: fans at the Dessert Gallery page, Facebook users who were not fans, and customers who were not active on Facebook. The individual data was compared with clients from the first survey who had become fans of Dessert Gallery on Facebook.

It turned out that the Facebook customers' behavior was influenced in a positive way. People who had responded to both surveys and had become fans were the best customers of Dessert Gallery. Although they spent about the same amount of money each visit, the number of store visits increased as they shared the Dessert Gallery information in a positive way with their friends on Facebook.

The Dessert Gallery fans frequented the store 20 percent more often than customers who had not joined the Facebook page. Dessert Gallery fans also showed more emotional involvement than non-fans (3.4 on a four-point scale, compared to 3.0 for other clients). Fans said they chose Dessert Gallery over other pastry shops in the area.

This research was on a small scale with small numbers. Only 283 (or 2.1 percent) of customers on the mailing list became fans of Dessert Gallery within three months. Still, that's not a bad result for a small store and it is only the beginning of what the future may bring in terms of customer loyalty and sales improvement. See if you can find 283 customers and motivate them to connect to your brand. They will be your new ambassadors, your biggest fans. Pamper them and give them something special they can share with their friends. Your network of satisfied customers will only increase. Think small, grow big.

Measure Success

How can you measure the success of your social media efforts? Follow the pointers on this list every week and you'll start to see results after a few months.

1. Measure how many visitors come to your website through Google Analytics.
2. Note the number of online comments posted by enthusiastic fans and customers.
3. Keep track of how many users visit your other digital channels.
4. Pay attention to rising sales figures. Ask customers where they've seen your brand.
5. Take screen shots of your Google search results.
6. Measure your increase in revenues from existing customers as a result of better service and attention.

Being active with social media has a big impact on your search engine results. The more people who tell each other about your business, the more powerful your brand will be. A typical Google search will show numerous results from a wide variety of sources. In addition to websites, YouTube videos and relevant images will also appear with the results. Companies that efficiently organize their digital content will make sure that all the videos on their website are also posted on YouTube and Facebook.

Include the URL of your website in the description or title of each video and tag them with keywords which you want to be found. The same goes for your pictures: instead of naming a photo "0345.jpg," call it "HP_monitor1907_www.maplin_uk_.jpg." This will make it much easier for people to find your content when they do general searches about the types of products or services you sell.

Google is a friend to those who place their content on different databases. Marketing professionals who remember that and post content on to all their networks will be rewarded with better online traffic. That, combined with a dialogue with your customers, will help any company succeed.

CHAPTER 12

DIALOGUE MARKETING

"Monitor, engage, and be transparent; these have always been the keys to success in the digital space." —Dallas Lawrence, Levick Strategic Communications

SOCIAL MEDIA PRESENTS A UNIQUE OPPOR-tunity to keep abreast with your audience. You can ask questions and receive immediate feedback from your biggest fans via Twitter, Facebook, and LinkedIn. While traditional market research will always remain qualitative and face-to-face interviews will give you additional valuable information that cannot be measured online, these types of research are costly. Sometimes you just want to know what your customers think about a new idea or service that you plan to develop. Here again, you already need to start telling your story, or rather, a new chapter in the story about your business. Share your thoughts and ideas for improving your service plan and ask for feedback from your fans, followers, and customers.

Of course, not all your current customers are on your Facebook page, and only the pioneers follow you on Twitter. But the world changes and the next generation, which has grown up with web 2.0, is much more intuitive to responding online and accustomed to giving their opinion, solicited or not. The customer now has power over your online reputation.

Before you know it, you might read a negative story about your business online that tops search engine results, all because you had a dispute with a customer. Once upon a time, you could live with that because "you can't make everybody happy." Today you have to be alert and go that extra mile for your current customers with a simple thing called attention. Pay attention to customers' opinions and questions. All customers want to feel that you care about them and that their opinion is valued.

A great technique that Tim Ellis discovered for JuniorSenior two years ago at InterlinkONE in Boston is the Purl, or Personal URL. Through a letter or an email, customers can be invited to a personalized website. The name of the web address has to be creative, must hold a promise, and should appeal to the imagination. The name is followed by the URL, e.g. `abkuijer.getsafreeholiday.com`. People are curious by nature, and the recipient will be more responsive to the link because you have personalized the web address.

One example of a company that successfully employed this is the Cultural Youth Passport Organization (CJP) in the Netherlands. They wanted to inform their partners, such as museums, music venues, and theaters, about the availability of a new "Culture Card" for young people between the ages of 12 and 18. It was a program, run by CJP, which allowed teens interested in art to visit museums, theaters, galleries, and music halls in the area. CJP sent out offers for personalized URLs like `TheatreMetropolis.wantsnewvisitors.com` so that these partners could learn about the offer in a unique way.

CJP grabbed recipients' attention with the personalization and the promise in the URL. They followed the link and landed on a special page with information specific to their company. CJP wanted to inform and get feedback on the new website, as well as verify that the correct contact person had been approached. Although the response to regular newsletters was already high (about 30 percent), they decided to try the Purl technique to start up a dialogue with their partners on a more personal basis. A postcard invitation with a Purl resulted in a staggering 71 percent response, proof that personal attention in combination with smart technology works.

Telling Tales

I spoke in an earlier chapter about the importance of companies selling their brands through storytelling. To recap, the trick is to tell stories in the right way. I do not mean using proper intonation and pronunciation, but telling a story that is honest, fair, and interactive. Now that we've covered the various social networks, you can see through this next example how to tell stories using these networks to gain a following.

Last year I spoke to an entrepreneur that wanted to build a car wash in a historic part of a small city.

The building permit process did not go smoothly because the local residents objected, thinking that the car wash would create a lot of noise pollution. "And to think I invested in the latest equipment with the lowest noise level and super-efficient water consumption," sighed the man. I advised him to tell his story from the beginning, to all concerned, about his dream to build that car wash. I told him, "Grab a video camera, set it up on a tripod on-site, and record your weekly story and progress. Explain how quiet, economical, and modern the machine is, that it will be turned off every night at closing time. Set their minds at ease. Show your commitment. Be human and be open to dialogue. Upload a video to YouTube every week."

The man hesitated. The idea appealed to him, but he was nervous to put himself in the public eye and tell such a personal story. I understand such a reaction—it is a big step as an entrepreneur to show your emotions. Yet personal branding is becoming increasingly important: people like real stories from real people instead of a folder full of rhetorical twaddle from an advertising agency. "And how will I get viewers?" he wanted to know.

I told him:

> To get the initial viewers you need a flywheel; the first 100 visitors are essential. If the subject appeals to them, then they will send the movie on to their friends and neighbors who don't like washing their cars by hand. The easiest way to capture viewers is through the use of a popular media type: the old-fashioned flyer. Put a pamphlet in the mailbox of all residents in a ten-street radius and mention that you plan to upload a new video on your "Car Wash on Main Street" YouTube channel every Saturday.

> That way you start informing people about the car wash and can invite them to ask questions. Open the dialogue. You can address new feedback in each subsequent broadcast. By the time the car wash opens, you will probably have gathered a few thousand fans. Your Google reputation and ranking grows in a natural way, because months prior to opening, your story was already told and shared online by the locals, your primary target.

> They can become members of your Facebook page in exchange for a free car wash, and on the opening day treat all your virtual contacts to a drink and give them additional discounts in the first week. I would place one advertisement in the newspaper, and spend the rest of your advertising budget on your first 500 clients.

The man thought it was a good idea and said he would think about it. The whole approach sounded a bit too revolutionary and was very different from what he was used to. People need time to adjust to change, especially in the field of communications. Only a few are willing to take a risk and do something out of the ordinary.

Each company has a story to tell. Claranor is a company based in Avignon, France, which produces machines that can sterilize water bottle caps with laser light. With a high-powered light beam that lasts a nano-second, micro bacteria in the caps are destroyed. This method is clean, fast, and better than current techniques using chlorine, water, and UV light. These are sufficient ingredients for a good story, or so you would think, but most people would be bored to tears after a few minutes of listening to the specifics of the process. Fortunately, there are many laser-light engineers and microbiologists online; the challenge is to find them to tell your story. By searching the right networks for the appropriate contacts, in this case food scientists, laser-light engineers, and microbiologists, you can easily tell your story and get a significant response.

In this case, the marketing manager became a member of these groups and asked colleagues from the laboratory to do the same. Posts and threads were started. The company's online presence grew and branding rose. In this way, they garnered increased respect for and awareness of their company within their community about a very specific issue. By using a social media strategy, they were able to get almost 250 participants for a webinar about their environmentally-friendly revolution.

True stories: you could write a book about them. But it's even better to distribute them online through dialogue marketing and social networks.

CHAPTER 13

THINK SMALL, GROW BIG

"Think Small, Grow Big." —Ab Kuijer, Social Media Activist

THANKS TO THE WONDERFUL WORLD OF advertising, an ever-growing consumer society has been created that is continually tempted into buying. Nowadays it is quite normal to have three televisions, two cars, and the latest Japanese designer jeans. You eat out twice a week and go on vacation four times a year (they are basically just long weekends away, you know).

We also have to drink crystal water from the Andes, stand in line for hours to buy the latest version of the iPad, drink Nescafé coffee packaged in funky-colored capsules. We live in a society that is becoming increasingly crazy, where we have so many choices as to what we can buy that more and more people are going "back to the basics," taking vacations where they walk through the desert to get back to true reality and the meaning of life. Our children have an average of 3,000 dollars worth of items in their rooms, from video game consoles to televisions, computers, and MP3 players. And so it continues. One new gadget is hardly out when we are already looking forward to the next one, this time with a five-inch screen or better speakers or an integrated solar panel.

Consumerism has taken hold of everyone, and yet no one questions how we can spend less money but buy more stuff. Just look at the price of an LCD TV—over the last five years, the price has dramatically fallen. For less than 800 dollars, you can buy a huge TV—you could almost open a small theater! A flat pack bookcase only costs 40 dollars, complete with hundreds of screws, something to assemble on a Sunday afternoon.

Everything seems to be cheap and useful, but think of where it has come from; more than likely produced for next to nothing in some far-off country. Even though we are not aware of it, something has definitely gone wrong. The online video "The Story of Stuff" shows us in simple terms why things have gone wrong and how you can help to change this.

I know this all runs counter to the contents of this book, helping marketing professionals to better communicate their message in order to sell more, but sometimes I wish we could be happy with what we have and that we would only feel obligated to consume when something needs to be replaced. And that we would choose to remain loyal to specific brands, and that those brands would make us feel important. Okay, I'm a dreamer, but that's not so bad, right?

My last tip for a better world: `www.storyofstuff.com`.

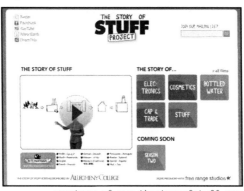

courtesy of www.thestoryofstuff.com

THE SOCIAL MEDIA FIVE-STEP PLAN

THE SOCIAL MEDIA FIVE-STEP PLAN IS SOMEthing that any marketer or advertiser can implement to easily get into the social networking arena without feeling overwhelmed. This plan details the five basic steps any advertiser should take when entering the social media platform, and if done effectively, will help gain online ambassadors that will essentially do your work for you. If you've read all the previous chapters, then you know how important it is to start small, paying attention to your current customers in order to get more great clients just like them through the networks they already frequent: namely Facebook, Twitter, and LinkedIn. This simple five-step process will guide you through using what you already have in order to build a larger platform that you can dialogue with and learn from while increasing your sales and brand awareness.

Step 1: Dip into the network of someone else first.

There are thousands of online networks of which your business contacts and suppliers are members. After all, man remains a social animal and is always looking for kindred spirits. Do not forget to look at your competitors and see what they are doing in the virtual world. There are sub-networks for accountants, logistics service providers, digital printers, microbiologists, or nuclear researchers. Every profession has its own network, forum, or online group. Read about the current topics of interest on the forums related to your business or clients. It is important to become a member of several networks and to participate in a discussion at least once a month, either by asking questions or launching discussions.

The interest in space technology, fly fishing, snowboarding, model trains, or routers surpasses all age barriers and wallets; it is the shared passion and interest of these groups that brings users together. Ultimately, everyone has their own network. And if your news is relevant, inspiring, and interesting, your customers are most likely willing to share that with their peers. Often this is their role within a network where friends and acquaintances always comment: "Wow, you're always up to date with all the latest things, how do you do that?"

It is important to sort out your business contacts. Who do you know, in which networks do they operate, and to what groups do they belong? A good starting point for a dialogue with people you trust is to ask them a question and listen to the answer. Consult your current address book that has information about your existing clients, suppliers, friends, and peers. Find those who will engage you and introduce you into their network. The number of contacts you have isn't what counts, but the quality of those who help you.

Step 2: Activate your new accounts.

To manage your social media activities properly, open a free Gmail account and use that email address for all your new accounts on the networks of your peers. If you are the owner of the company, display a picture of yourself with the logo in the background. Don't hide behind your logo, people want to do business with a real person. Tony Hsieh is the CEO of Zappos, the largest online shoe store in the U.S., and he has become a national icon because he is the face of his store and promotes his business with passion and creativity. He keeps his customers abreast of his interests and activities via his Twitter account, which has almost two million followers.

You should use the same account name on all networks. Make sure the desired name is still available and register it on all the sites you want to belong to. This may seem like a chore now, but view it as an investment in the future. At the back of this book you'll find links to helpful websites for a digital name-check.

Use Google Documents to create and save Word files. It is wise to record all log-in details, such as the name of the network, web address, username, and password in a secure Word document from day one. Using Gmail, you can consult or update this document from anywhere in the world. Ask your communications department to share the login data with key individuals in the organization so everyone involved is free to make reports on weekly social media activities.

Once you've become a member of networks like LinkedIn, Facebook, Xing, Viadeo, and Twitter, start looking for keywords that relate to your business. With these keywords, you can find online groups where people discuss your specialty. Sign up for all these groups, but do nothing for the first week. Read what's being offered, become familiar with the etiquette, and learn from the trendsetters—the people with the most knowledge and the largest network.

As you become more familiar with each network, the time will come to start actively participating in discussions, preferably ones where the trendsetters are active. Be constructive, friendly, give advice, and most importantly, do not sell! Be relaxed, just like you would be at any social event where most of the guests do not know you. You would never charge in selling your product right away. You would listen to the stories of others, and only when you know enough about them would you connect with them regarding issues in your field. You might give them a customized offer, and only when you were certain they were open to it. The same holds true for online groups. Do not rush headlong into brow-beating other members into buying the offer of the week, tooting your own horn, otherwise you won't keep your foot in the virtual door for long.

Step 3: Start your first social media channel.

Now that you've studied virtual networks on existing channels, it is time to set up your own social media channel. Of course, you can generate a customer forum and post a newsletter on your company website, but that's like having a store in the middle of nowhere while everyone is shopping in the mall two miles away. Be realistic and efficient and open a page on Facebook.

With more than 650 million users and over 1.6 million pages of corporate information, this forum is a proven success. Collectively, Facebook pages can reach over five billion people. And it's completely free. There are numerous studies showing that people who "Like" the Facebook page of a particular brand will spend more than the average customer. Another added benefit of a page is that the average click-through rate on a commercial link is almost seven percent. Compare that with the average 0.00004 percent click-ratio on an advertising banner.

If you do not have the time to manage your Facebook page and review comments and questions yourself, entrust the responsibility to a member of your customer service team, someone who has sufficient experience in speaking and writing in a serious, passionate, and enthusiastic way.

Many companies tell their marketing manager to work on social media as part of their main activities. That's easier said than done. Social media requires a different approach to marketing. It's not about media planning and evaluating creative messages from an external advertising agency, it is all about storytelling.

If the intentions of the company can be clearly communicated, and the promise to the customer is strong, then you can start to communicate on social media. From here on in, it is the dialogue with the customer and the realization that every customer, no matter how small, is of the utmost importance. Invite each shop visitor or passerby to join your online community. Do not spam them with advertisements, but listen to them, and see what they think about your product. Before you launch a new product, make sure the world knows what efforts your company made to launch it. It is not the destination, but the journey, that counts.

Step 4: Dedicate your employees to upholding your online image.

Now that the company has been registered with the various networks, and the Facebook page is active, it is time to mobilize your own people. Send an internal newsletter to all staff and invite them to join the Facebook page. Reward them for joining with an extra incentive, like a copywriting course or another suitable job within the company. Look for the "digital natives" in your business. Find out who is active on a daily or weekly basis on Twitter and Facebook. Invite these people to join the Digital Task Force, to start tweeting and posting about your business.

If you allow people to blog online or tweet during work hours, then, as a prerequisite, you should get a commitment from the staff that everyone writes positively about the company at least once a week. There can even be a reward for the best performance, such as a month's salary or extra vacation time.

This way, you motivate staff and build the company's virtual reputation together. It is also beneficial in that the more people who write about your product and business and link back to your website, the better the search engine results will be.

Step 5: Keep up with your networks daily.

Now it is important to work on a plan for scheduling your social media activities Post an article and see which day scores best with hits on the website or retweets. Within a few weeks of starting down the social media path, following the new strategy of think small, grow big, you should develop a logical process for your different social media activities:

1. Select the most important issues to post as news.
2. Formulate new discussions to get feedback.
3. Scan the Internet for mentions of your business or service.
4. Respond to questions and jump in on threads that are negative.

It is not necessary to log in to all your networks each time you want to update. Using an RSS (Really Simple Syndication) feed simplifies this task. Any news that is posted on the site can be equipped with an RSS feed that can be placed on various other digital channels such as your Facebook page, Twitter, or LinkedIn accounts. This ensures that your news is automatically updated in numerous locations at once, exactly as you want.

For any business, the website must change weekly. You will

never score highly on search engines if you have static content on the homepage. Dead websites with text from brochures and a contact form need the help of an SEO agency to get ahead in the search engines.

Using Google AdWords and link optimization, you can easily spend a few thousand dollars per month and still not get fantastic results. It is more natural to upload something every week in a blog on your homepage dealing with your work, your passion, your company, your employees, and your customers.

Make the keywords in your text bold and you will see almost real-time improvements in your results on Google. There are many more tricks that you can find online. Too much work? Think of it as an investment in yourself and as a great opportunity to learn something new.

By following this social media five-step plan, any marketer and advertiser can make the most of social networks to boost sales and build customer relationships. Marketers who build their online reputation while keeping in mind the main principles of the "think small, grow big" mindset—putting the customer first; paying attention to all customers, no matter how small; dialoguing with and learning from the consumer; telling a story instead of hard selling to make an impact—will see positive results and can be confident that their business is one which will satisfy customers for years to come.

10 STEPS TO CREATING A SOCIAL MEDIA POLICY FOR YOUR COMPANY

M ANY COMPANIES ARE WARY OF GIVING too much online freedom to their employees. The establishment of a social media regulation document makes the possibilities and expectations clear. Of course, it is not without its risks. Employees can get your company in trouble by tweeting sensitive information while you are struggling with a "politically correct" official press release, or someone in your organization might respond inappropriately to messages from third parties. It is important that you formulate the rules for your business. The Marketing Zen Group in Dallas, Texas, has a clear ten-step plan for implementing a social media policy[2]:

> *1) Decide where you stand.* A policy is only as good as the company that implements it. Essentially, the lines are drawn and you have to take a stand. How far is your company willing to go in the social media sphere? Will you choose to only communicate in reaction to what someone else

says? Will you be proactive in engaging the community (consumers and bloggers)? Without an overall attitude about social media, it can be very hard to create a policy.

2) *Determine what constitutes social media.* While a blog and LinkedIn may easily be categorized as social media—what about online video? What about Twitter? What really constitutes social media? You must have your own (preferably) written definition. This is especially true because new websites and tools emerge all the time. My personal definition of social media is any website or medium (including video) which allows for communication in the open.

3) *Clarify who owns what.* Does your company have a Facebook page that is handled by the head of HR? What happens when that person leaves? Who owns that page? That content? James C. Roberts III of Global Capital Group Law offers this: "If there is an offer letter or employment contract, it would normally state who owns what (usually the company). Absent that, the law could default to ownership by the company (but depending upon the state). On the other hand, if the company has turned a blind eye to personal use during work hours then it could be attacked. And, it will depend upon the extent to which what is created is based on company property (IP)." (This is not to be construed as legal advice. Please consult with your own attorneys for such.) To keep things simple, make sure you and your employees know what is theirs and what belongs to the company.

4) *Keep confidential information private.* While other policies may address the issue of keeping proprietary and personal information confidential—it never hurts to readdress it in terms of social networking. Due to the casual nature of these sites, it is easier to give away key information without realizing it. Even private messages aren't always secure. Each site is has its own fallibilities. Best to just never share any confidential or proprietary information using social media—publicly or privately.

5) *Decide who is responsible.* While it is important that everyone understands the company's social media policy, it is also important that one person or a team of people be responsible for managing social media efforts. If a customer does make a public complaint—who will answer it? Do they need to forward that to another department? Social media doesn't automatically fall under the job description of the web developer, PR person, or HR manager, etc. All employees should be encouraged to interact and represent the brand, but there should be one or a few who are proactively handling queries. The best way to find a social media advocate within the company is to seek out the one person or team of people who are most passionate about communicating with customers in such a manner. They may already be doing so without you knowing it. Seek those people out and train them well.

6) *Dictate the rules of engagement—without being a dictator.* It is a fine line to walk—allowing employees the freedom to engage and protecting

the company at the same time. However, it can be done. You can't stop employees from communicating using the new mediums but you can set some ground rules that work for everybody's benefit. Take a look at Intel's social media policy: `www.intel.com/sites/sitewide/en_US/social-media.htm`. The Emerging Technology Department at the Air Force (yes, they have one!) has created this flow chart of their own guidelines: ~~`http://blogcouncil.org/blog/wp-content/uploads/2008/12/air-force-blog-assessment.jpg`~~. [The link is dead—sorry!]

7) *Address taboo topics.* While your employees probably already exercise good common sense while participating online, it never hurts to clarify specifically what is off limits. Raj Malik of Network Solutions offers this partial list:

   a. Topics in which The Company is involved in litigation or could in the future: (i.e. policy, customer disputes, etc.)

   b. Non-public information of any kind about The Company, including, but not limited to, policies and strategy

   c. Illegal or banned substances and narcotics

   d. Pornography or other offensive illegal materials

   e. Defamatory, libelous, offensive or demeaning material

   f. Private/Personal matters of yourself or others

   g. Disparaging/threatening comments about or related to anyone

   h. Personal, sensitive or confidential information of any kind

8) Have a system for monitoring the social sphere. A social media policy doesn't do much good if you don't actually monitor the space where the conversation is happening. There are plenty of free and paid tools to monitor the online space. There are also firms like ours that offer reputation management services. You can read about some of the reputation management tools available [here: http://www.marketingzen.com/reputation-management-the-other-side-of-social-media-marketing/].

9) Make training easily available. Think win-win. Nobody likes to be bossed around—especially when it comes to their own social networking. However, most people are very open to learning about how to better leverage these sites to further their own careers and brands. Most people who make mistakes online just don't know any better. If you expect your employees to utilize the social networking tools properly, you must provide training. What they put out there isn't just a reflection of the company; it is also a reflection of them. Make it a win-win for everybody.

10) Have a Crisis Plan. Let's say you have a perfect social media policy in place, what happens if an employee breeches it? What happens if the people you laid off decide to start a Facebook hate group? Or, if a disgruntled customer creates a YouTube video (hey, it happened to United Airlines!)? The worst action is inaction. You must act immediately if a crisis occurs. Ignoring it or worse—trying to bury it—will only increase the backlash. This is given that the mistake was truly yours. I am not referring to wild accusations or remarks that have no basis. Ideally, you have already been proactive in your efforts. You have a company blog, you have a twitter account, and you have some influencers as friends who will vouch for your company. Either way, you will need to take corrective action right away. First, contact the person responsible. Apologize, clarify—and do what you need to in order to rectify the mistake. Second, make a public announcement apologizing and clarifying. Also, address steps put into place that will keep such a debacle from occurring again. In social media, transparency is crucial. This is why step # 1 is, well, step #1—decide where you stand.

TIPS & LINKS

An easy way to make a quick video on YouTube: Upload photos of your fleet and your employees, find some suitable music, and within two minutes you have a movie you can post on YouTube. `www.animoto.com`

Social Business Cards: Do not forget to put your LinkedIn profile and your Twitter account on your new business cards. Show your customers that your company is innovative.

Facebook Tips

12 Applications to Make Your Facebook Page More Engaging | Social Media Today
`www.socialmediatoday.com/SMC/197503?utm_source=smt_newsletter&utm_medium=email&utm_campaign=newsletter`

9 Ways to Enhance Your Facebook Fan Page | Social Media Examiner
`www.socialmediaexaminer.com/9-ways-to-enhance-your-facebook-fan-Pagina`

How to Get Thousands of Facebook Fans With A Single Video | AllFacebook.com
www.allfacebook.com/2009/11/how-to-get-thousands-of-facebook-fans-with-a-single-video

4 Facebook Apps That Add Professionalism to Your Profile | CIO.com—Business Technology Leadership
www.cio.com/article/590765/4_Facebook_Apps_That_Add_Professionalism_to_Your_Profile?source=CIONLE_nlt_insider_2010-04-15

Twitter Tips

Counting number of Tweets real-time | Popacular.com
popacular.com/gigatweet

8 Useful Tips to Become Successful With Twitter | Smashing Magazine
www.smashingmagazine.com/2009/02/03/8-useful-tips-to-become-successul-with-twitter

12 Tips to Engage People on Twitter | Social Media Examiner
www.socialmediaexaminer.com/12-tips-to-engage-people-on-twitter

A Twitter Guide to Handling Anything Your Customers Throw at You | MarketingVOX
www.marketingvox.com/a-twitter-guide-to-handling-anything-your-customers-throw-at-you-046850

LinkedIn Tips

How to use your LinkedIn | INC.com
`www.inc.com/maisha-walker/2009/08/how_to_use_your_`
`linkedin_profi.html`

10 LinkedIn tips for professionals | Ian Brodie
`www.ianbrodie.com/marketing/linkedin-tips-`
`professionals`

7 Ways to Get More Out of LinkedIn | Mashable
`mashable.com/2009/11/09/linkedin-tips`

10 LinkedIn Tips to optimize your profile | Seoptimise
www.seoptimise.com/blog/2009/09/10-tips-to-optimise-your-linkedin-profile.html

Check the name of your new digital identity:

www.namechecklist.com

www.ud.com

knowem.com

claim.io/welcome

www.tm.biz

namechk.com

domai.nr

Software for social media measurement:

www.ubervu.com

www.viralheat.com

www.socialmention.com

www.postrank.com

www.bloglines.com

blogsearch.google.com

www.trackur.com

www.oneriot.com

socialmedia.alterian.com

www.radian6.com

If you need serious online support:

The Social Media Army

www.jr-sr.com/nl/social-media-army

ABOUT THE AUTHOR

AB KUIJER is a (social) media activist. He has broad experience in the communication field in all types of media. He has been a journalist in the Netherlands (PCM, Telegraaf), radio host (Decibel, WAPS), feature film producer (Castings), television producer (Veronica, BNN), thinker, writer, and blogger (abkuijer.com). He is the founder and creative director of international communication agency JuniorSenior. Ab was elected Europe's Best Youth Marketing Expert in 2010 by the Youth Research Partners. He also won an award from Esprix in 1997 for Effective Communication and the European Excellence Award in 2008 for an outstanding PR campaign with Hertz. He frequently gives lectures and workshops on the innovation and application of social media. When Ab is not traveling, he spends his life with his family and friends in the south of France. You can visit him online at `www.abkuijer.com`.

COSIMO is a specialty publisher of books and publications that inspire, inform, and engage readers. Our mission is to offer unique books to niche audiences around the world.

COSIMO BOOKS publishes books and publications for innovative authors, nonprofit organizations, and businesses.

COSIMO BOOKS specializes in bringing books back into print, publishing new books quickly and effectively, and making these publications available to readers around the world.

COSIMO CLASSICS offers a collection of distinctive titles by the great authors and thinkers throughout the ages.

At **COSIMO CLASSICS** timeless works find new life as affordable books, covering a variety of subjects including: Business, Economics, History, Personal Development, Philosophy, Religion & Spirituality, and much more!

COSIMO REPORTS publishes public reports that affect your world, from global trends to the economy, and from health to geopolitics.

FOR MORE INFORMATION CONTACT US AT
INFO@COSIMOBOOKS.COM

➢ if you are a book lover interested in our current catalog of books

➢ if you represent a bookstore, book club, or anyone else interested in special discounts for bulk purchases

➢ if you are an author who wants to get published

➢ if you represent an organization or business seeking to publish books and other publications for your members, donors, or customers.

**COSIMO BOOKS ARE ALWAYS
AVAILABLE AT ONLINE BOOKSTORES**

**VISIT COSIMOBOOKS.COM
BE INSPIRED, BE INFORMED**

9 781616 405403